Exploring Science

MW00892533

Daily Science Workbook
for kids in Grades 4-5 To
Master the Subject and
Ace the Tests!

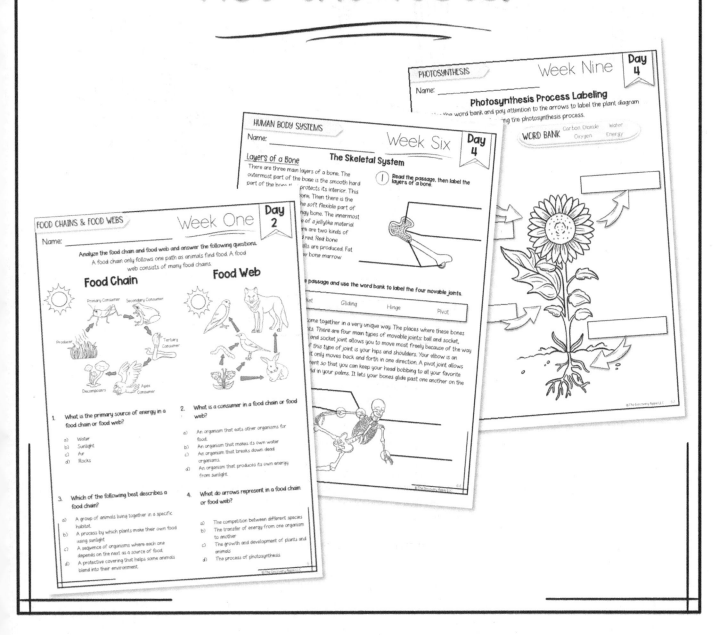

Written by Fatema Ghazi
Illustrations by Mariam Ghazi

Contact the author:
Fatema@thediscoveryapple.com

Workbook Highlights

WEEKLY TOPICS

Each week focuses on a different science topic, such as plant life cycle, animal adaptations, the human body, etc.

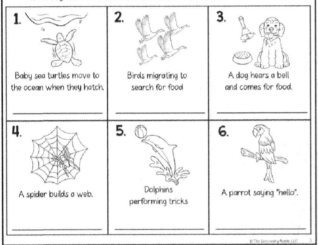

DAILY WORKSHEETS

Each topic consists of five worksheets, one for each weekday.

VARIETY OF ACTIVITIES

Each topic is explored through different types of activities:

- Reading Comprehension: Students read passages related to the topic and answer questions to demonstrate their understanding.
- Vocabulary: Activities focus on building and reinforcing vocabulary related to the topic, helping students grasp important scientific terms and concepts.
- Labeling Diagrams: Students practice identifying and labeling parts of diagrams or illustrations related to the topic, enhancing their understanding of its components.
- Critical Thinking Writing Response: Students are prompted to think critically about the topic and express their ideas through writing. These prompts encourage them to analyze, evaluate, and reflect on what they've learned, fostering higher-order thinking skills and creativity.

REVIEW AND REINFORCEMENT

Can be used as review and reinforcement of key concepts. You can use it alongside their regular science curriculum to deepen their understanding of daily life science topics.

FLEXIBLE USE

Can be used in various ways, such as for homework assignments, independent study, or as part of a classroom lesson. It can also serve as a tool for assessment and progress tracking.

Table of Contents

THIS BOOK BELONGS TO:

_____

Food Chains and Food Webs

Every creature depends on each other for food. It's like a wild game of Jenga — once one piece is gone, the rest start to wobble!

Name: _____

Week One

Read the passage, then label the organisms.

All living things have important roles in ecosystems and rely on each other as part of the food chain. A food chain describes how living organisms get their energy and nutrients for survival. Producers, consumers, and decomposers make up the different links in this chain, based on what they eat and how they contribute to the energy of the ecosystem.

Plants produce energy through photosynthesis, so they are considered **producers**. Consumers, such as animals, do not produce energy; instead, they obtain energy by consuming other organisms. Animals that eat other animals are called **carnivores**. **Herbivores** eat only plants and **Omnivores** eat both plants and animals. **Decomposers** break down dead plants and animals into nutrients that can be used by other living things.

All living things work together to keep ecosystems healthy and balanced.

Identify and label each organism.

WORD BANK

Carnivore   Producer   Herbivore   Omnivore   Decomposer

1.

Rabbits eat grass and hay.

_____

2.

Earthworms break down dead plants and animals

_____

3.

Brown bears eat plants, berries, fish and insects

_____

4.

Snakes eat other animals and sometimes other snakes.

_____

5.

Lions mainly eat meat.

_____

6.

Sunflowers make their food through photosynthesis.

_____

7.

Giraffes eat leaves, buds, and twigs from trees.

_____

8.

Mushrooms break down dead leaves, wood, and plant debris.

_____

Name: _____

Analyze the food chain and food web and answer the following questions.

Food Chain

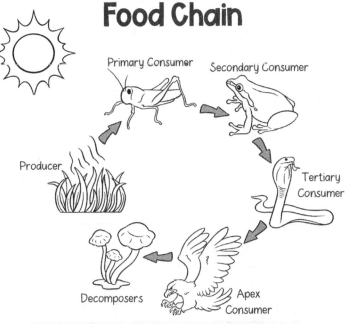

A food chain only follows one path as animals find food.

Food Web

A food web consists of many food chains.

1. **What is the primary source of energy in a food chain or food web?**

   a) Water
   b) Sunlight
   c) Air
   d) Rocks

2. **What is a consumer in a food chain or food web?**

   a) An organism that eats other organisms for food.
   b) An organism that makes its own water
   c) An organism that breaks down dead organisms.
   d) An organism that produces its own energy from sunlight.

3. **Which of the following best describes a food chain?**

   a) A group of animals living together in a specific habitat.
   b) A process by which plants make their own food using sunlight
   c) A sequence of organisms where each one depends on the next as a source of food.
   d) A protective covering that helps some animals blend into their environment.

4. **What do arrows represent in a food chain or food web?**

   a) The competition between different species
   b) The transfer of energy from one organism to another
   c) The growth and development of plants and animals
   d) The process of photosynthesis

Name: _____

Vocab Match

Match each word with its definition. Write the correct letter in the space provided.

1. Producer _____

2. Omnivore _____

3. Herbivore _____

4. Carnivore _____

5. Decomposers _____

A) An consumer that eats only other animals

B) A consumer that eats both plants and animals

C) A consumer that eats only plants

D) An organism that makes its own food through photosynthesis

E) An organism that breaks down dead plants and animals into simpler substances

6. Fill in the chart below.

Herbivores	Carnivores	Omnivores	Decomposers
List 2 examples	List 2 examples	List 2 examples	List 2 examples
☆	☆	☆	☆
☆	☆	☆	☆
Illustrate the foods they eat	Illustrate the foods they eat	Illustrate the foods they eat	Illustrate the foods they eat

Name: _____

Exploring a Food Web

Use the food web below to answer the questions.

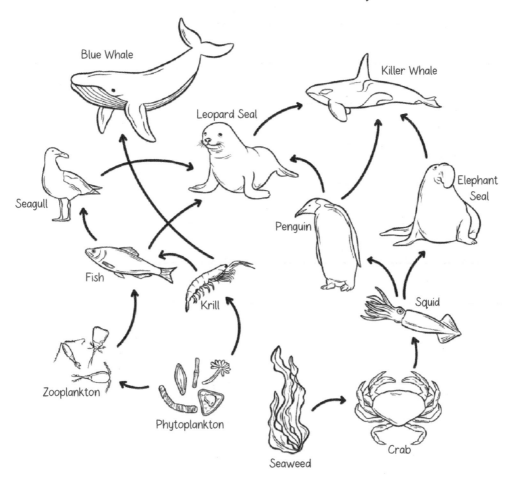

1. What are the producers in this food web?

2. How many food chains can you find in this food web?

3. What are the top consumers in this food web?

Week One

Name: _____

Why do you think a disruption in one part of a food chain or food web can affect other organisms? Explain.

Biomes

In the Amazon rainforest, there are more species of plants and animals than anywhere else on Earth. But, did you know that scientists are still discovering new species every day?

Name: _____

Week Two

The Fascinating World of Biomes

Biomes are large regions on Earth where the climate, plants, and animals share similarities. For example, a desert biome is sandy, hot, and dry with very little to no rainfall. The tropical rainforest biome includes tall trees, high temperatures, and lots of rainfall throughout the year. The rainforest is home to a variety of animals such as monkeys and colorful birds.

Earth is home to various biomes. Each biome provides a habitat for plants and animals that have adapted to its particular environmental conditions. Can you identify the 6 biomes below?

Identify and label each biome.

WORD BANK

Rainforest   Tundra

Desert   Marine   Grassland   Freshwater

1. The coldest biome

_____

2. Includes many tall trees and high rainfall

_____

3. The biggest biome covering about 70% of the Earth

_____

4. The driest biome on Earth

_____

5. Includes rivers, lakes, and ponds

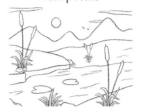

_____

6. Large and very flat areas covered in grass

_____

Name: _____

Research different biomes and answer the questions below.

1. Which biome is known for its tall trees that lose their leaves in the fall?

a) Rainforest
b) Desert
c) Tundra
d) Deciduous Forest

2. In which biome can you find blue whales and sharks?

a) Tundra
b) Marine
c) Freshwater
d) Desert

3. Which biome has lots of coniferous trees like pine and spruce?

a) Taiga
b) Tundra
c) Desert
d) Grassland.

4. Which biome is characterized by its vast grassy plains, with grazing animals like bison and zebras?

a) Rainforest
b) Desert
c) Grassland
d) Tundra .

5. Describe the <u>freshwater</u> biome. Include information about what types of plants and animals you might find and then illustrate it.

Describe it.	Draw it.
_____ _____ _____ _____ _____ _____ _____ _____ _____	

Name: _____

Match each word with its definition. Write the correct letter in the space provided.

1. Desert _____

2. Rainforest _____

3. Tundra _____

4. Grassland _____

5. Deciduous Forest _____

(A) a cold and icy biome found in the far north/ has a frozen ground called permafrost

(B) A dry and sandy or rocky place where it doesn't rain much

(C) goes through the four seasons/ trees lose their leaves at the end of each growing season

(D) wide open spaces with lots of grass and few trees

(E) a dense and lush forest found in warm regions with a lot of rainfall.

6. Compare and contrast tropical rainforests and temperate rainforests by listing their differences and similarities.

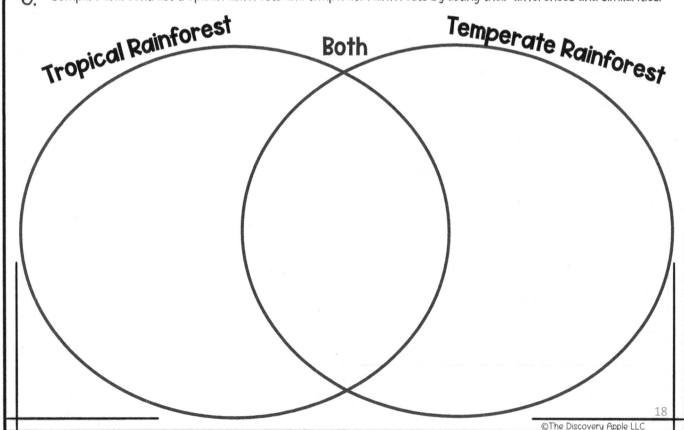

Tropical Rainforest   Both   Temperate Rainforest

Week Two

Name: _____

Color in the locations of the biomes.

1. Color in the locations of the tropical rainforests green.

2. Color in the locations of the deserts brown.

3. Color in the locations of the tundra orange

4. Color in the locations of the deciduous forests yellow

5. Color in the locations of the grasslands red

6. Color in the locations of the Taiga purple

If you were a scientist studying the desert biome, what questions would you want to investigate? What are some things you would like to learn about the plants, animals, or adaptations that help them survive in the desert?

Animal Adaptations

Animals are constantly adapting to changes in their environment.

Name: _____

Instinctive and Learned Behavior

Animal behaviors can be divided into two main categories: instinctive and learned. . Instinctive behaviors are those that animals are born with and perform automatically, without needing to be taught. For example, when a baby bird hatches from its egg, it knows instinctively how to open its mouth wide for food and how to chirp for its parents' attention.

On the other hand, learned behaviors are those that animals pick up over time through experience and observation. These behaviors are not automatic- they require practice. A dog learning to sit or fetch in response to commands from its owner is an example of learned behavior.

Both instinctive and learned behaviors are crucial for animals' survival and success in their environments.

Identify and label each animal behavior as instinctive or learned.

1.

Baby sea turtles move to the ocean when they hatch.
_____

2.

Birds migrating to search for food
_____

3.

A dog hears a bell and comes for food.
_____

4.

A spider builds a web.
_____

5.

Dolphins performing tricks
_____

6.

A parrot saying "hello".
_____

Week Three

Name: _____

Read the Passage and answer the questions.

Elephants

Did you know that elephants are the biggest land animals in the world? They can grow to eleven feet tall and weigh up to 13,000 pounds. Yikes! Elephants are known for their long, muscular trunks. Their long trunks are helpful to them in many ways. Their trunks can pick up food and move heavy objects. They also use it to suck up water for drinking or spray it over their body to cool off. In addition to water, elephants also throw dirt over their backs to protect them from the sun and the insects that bite.

Elephants have one tooth on each side of the upper jaw that form a tusk. It can measure up to eleven feet in length. They use their tusks for digging, fighting, and feeding. Elephants scrape bark off of trees using their tusks for food. It is also used as a resting place for the trunk.

Have you also noticed how big elephant ears are? Everything has a purpose in life, including elephant ears! When elephants get very hot, they flap their ears to create air currents across the ears and reduce extra body heat. Flapping your ears sounds like a fun way to cool off, don't you think? Because of the size of an elephant and their ivory tusks, hunters love to hunt them, which is why their population is decreasing.

Big Ears

Tusk

Trunk

1. What physical feature allows the elephant to dig, fight, and feed?

    _____

2. What physical feature allows the elephant to pick up food?

    _____

3. Why do elephants throw dirt over their backs?

    _____

    _____

4. What does it mean when elephants flap their big ears?

    _____

    _____

Week Three

Name: _____

Vocabulary Match

Match each word with its definition. Write the correct letter in the space provided.

1. Physical Adaptation _____

2. Behavioral Adaptation _____

3. Camouflage _____

4. Mimicry _____

5. Instinctive Behavior _____

6. Learned Behavior _____

7. Hibernation _____

8. Migration _____

9. Predator _____

10. Prey _____

A Behaviors that happen naturally

B When animals travel long trips to find warmer weather, food supply, and a safe place to give birth to their young

C Something an animal does or how it acts in order to stay alive

D An animal that is taken and eaten by another animal for food

E Looking or sounding like another living organism

F Behaviors taught through observation and experiencing their environment

G A visual disguise; When the color of an animal changes to look likes its surrounding

H A characteristic or change in an animals' body that helps it survive in its habitat

I An animal that hunts and eats other animals for food

J When an animal sleeps during the cold days of winter

24

Name: _____

Physical or Behavioral Adaptation

Physical and behavioral adaptations play important roles in helping organisms survive in their habitats.

Physical adaptations are special features or body parts the animals are born with that help them survive in their environment. For example, a giraffe has a long neck to reach high leaves for food.
Behavioral adaptations are things animals do to survive in their environment. For example, birds fly south for the winter to find warmer weather and more food

Classify whether each fact describes a physical or behavioral adaptation. Write physical or behavioral under each fact.

1.

Polar bears have thick fur to keep them warm.

_____

2.

A bird builds a nest to lay eggs.

_____

3.

Eagles have sharp claws to help them grasp prey

_____

4.

Butterflies migrate to find food

_____

5.

Fish travel in groups for protection

_____

6.

Penguins have webbed feet for efficient swimming in water.

_____

Name: _____

Some animals have unique ways of gathering or obtaining food. For example, woodpeckers use their beaks to drill into tree bark to find insects. Can you think of an animal with unique ways of getting food? How do their adaptations help them find or catch their food in their environments?

Animal Classification

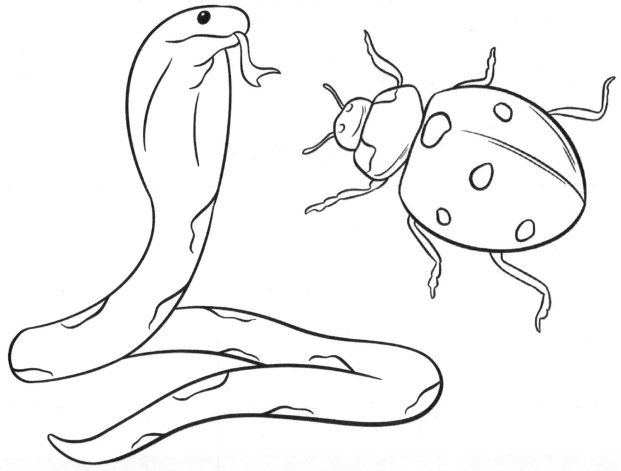

Classifying animals helps us understand the diversity of life on Earth.

Week Four

Name: _____

Categorizing Animals by Type

Mammals: Animals that have fur or hair, give birth to babies, and feed their young with milk. Humans are also mammals.

Birds: Animals with feathers, wings, beaks and two legs. They lay eggs.

Reptiles: Animals with scales, dry skin, and lay eggs on land. They can live in water or on land.

Amphibians: Animals that live both in water and on land, usually starting their lives in water as tadpoles and then growing into adults with legs. They lay their eggs in water.

Fish: Animals that live in water, breathe through gills, and have fins and scales.

Insects: Animals with six legs, a three-part body (head, thorax, abdomen), and often wings.

Classify each animal.

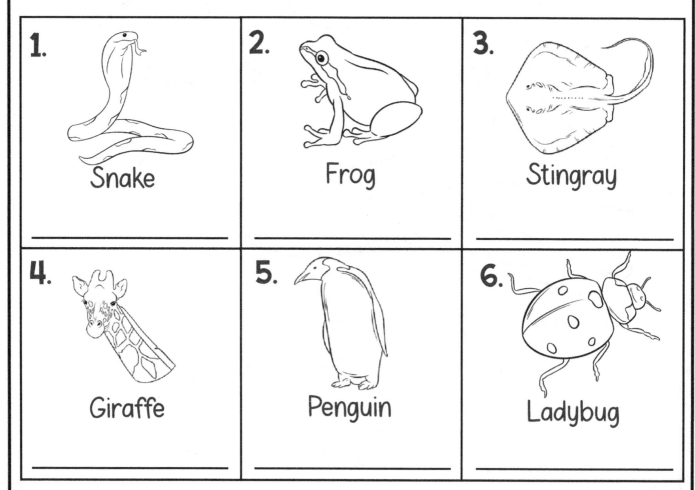

1. Snake

2. Frog

3. Stingray

4. Giraffe

5. Penguin

6. Ladybug

Week Four

Name: _____

Warm-Blooded and Cold-Blooded Animals

Warm-blooded and cold-blooded are terms used to describe how animals regulate their body temperature.

Warm-blooded animals are animals that maintain a constant body temperature regardless of the temperature outside Mammals and Birds are warm-blooded animals.

Cold-blooded animals' body temperature depends on whether it is hot or cold outside. Amphibians, reptiles, insects, and fish are cold-blooded animals.

List 5 warm-blooded animals and 5 cold-blooded animals in the chart below. Also, write what each animal is classified as (mammal, bird, reptile, amphibian, fish, or insect).

Warm-Blooded Animals	Cold-Blooded Animals
1.	1.
2.	2.
3.	3.
4.	4.
5.	5.

Week Four

Name: _____

Vocabulary Match

Match each word with its definition. Write the correct letter in the space provided.

1. Vertebrate _____

2. Invertebrate _____

3. Warm-blooded _____

4. Cold-blooded _____

5. Insect _____

6. Mammals _____

7. Amphibians _____

8. Reptiles _____

9. Fish _____

10. Bird _____

(A) The animal's body temperature depends on whether it is hot or cold outside
_____

(B) Warm-blooded vertebrate animals that feed its young with milk, have fur or hair, and breathe air with lungs.
_____

(C) Warm-blooded animals that lay eggs, have feathers, wings, and a beak
_____

(D) Animals that maintain a constant body temperature regardless of the temperature outside
_____

(E) Cold-blooded animals that breathe air and have scaly skin
_____

(F) An animal that has a spine or backbone
_____

(G) Cold-blooded invertebrate animals with three main body segments (head, thorax, and abdomen), six legs, and often wings.
_____

(H) Cold-blooded animals that live in water and has fins for swimming and gills for breathing

(I) An animal that does not have a spine or backbone
_____

(J) Cold-blooded vertebrate animals that live both in water and on land, usually starting their lives in water as tadpoles and then growing into adults with legs

Week Four

Name: _____

Vertebrate and Invertebrate Animals

Vertebrate animals are animals that have a backbone or spine. Mammals, birds, reptiles, amphibians, and fish are vertebrates.

Invertebrate animals are animals that DO NOT have a back bone or spine. Insects, worms, and jellyfish are invertebrates.

Classify whether each animal is considered a vertebrate or invertebrate animal. Write vertebrate or invertebrate under each picture.

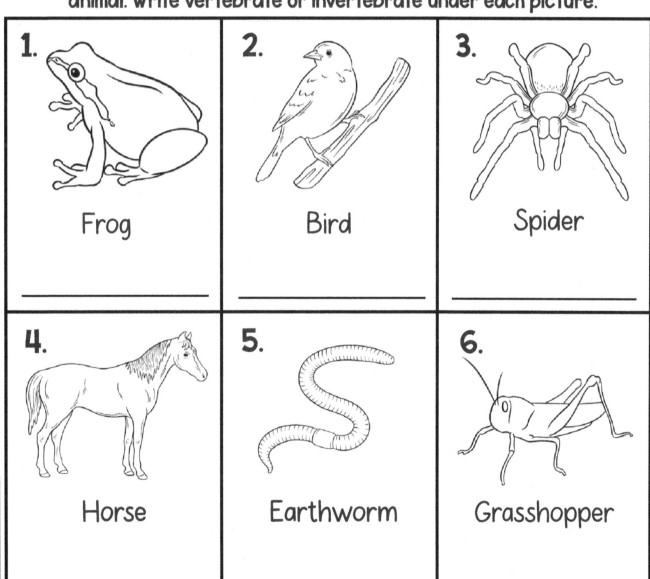

1.

Frog

_____

2.

Bird

_____

3.

Spider

_____

4.

Horse

_____

5.

Earthworm

_____

6.

Grasshopper

_____

Name: _____

Imagine you discover a new animal species while exploring a jungle and you begin to observe its physical features and behavior. Explain its physical characteristics and behavior, and classify it. Is it a mammal, bird, insect, fish, amphibian, or reptile? Is it warm-blooded or cold-blooded? Is it a vertebrate or invertebrate? Explain.

Draw the unique animal you described below.

Plant and Animal Cells

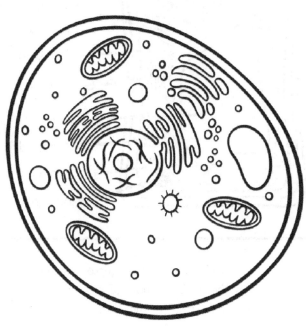

Plant cells have tiny green structures called chloroplasts that act like solar panels, turning sunlight into energy through photosynthesis.

Week Five

Examine the plant cell and read the passage. Use the passage to complete the tasks for the next few days.

Plant and Animal Cells

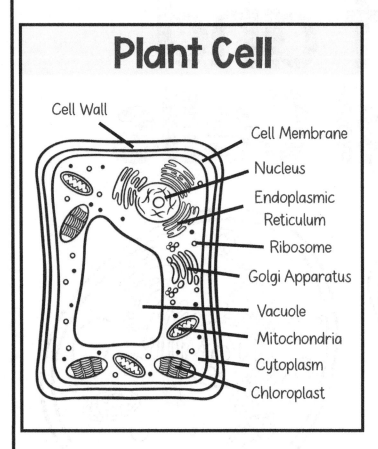

Plant Cell

- Cell Wall
- Cell Membrane
- Nucleus
- Endoplasmic Reticulum
- Ribosome
- Golgi Apparatus
- Vacuole
- Mitochondria
- Cytoplasm
- Chloroplast

Cells are the basic structure for all living organisms — animals and plants. Did you know that you are made up of cells? Cells are really tiny, so you need a microscope to be able to see them. A scientist named Robert Hook discovered and introduced cells to the world in 1665.

Both plant and animal cells are made up of organelles that perform specific jobs inside the cell. Organelles are protected and held inside a gel-like substance called cytoplasm. The cytoplasm contains fluids with fats, sugars, and acids that help keep the cell functioning. Examples of organelles include the nucleus, mitochondria, and endoplasmic reticulum.

The nucleus is what controls the activities of the cell. The nucleus is considered the "control center" of the cell. DNA is found in the nucleus which determines the characteristics of the organism, such as what the organism will look like. For example, the DNA can determine the size of a plant, or the eye color of an animal.

Plant and animal cells are surrounded by a cell membrane that protects the cell and controls what comes in and out of the cell. Both types of cells get their energy from the mitochondria, which is known as the powerhouse of the cell. The mitochondria takes in nutrients, breaks them down, and turns them into energy using molecules.

Vacuoles are the storage tanks that store water, food, and nutrients that the cell needs to survive. Vacuoles are found to be larger in plant cells than animal cells because they hold larger amounts of water. Cells also have a transportation network called the endoplasmic reticulum that takes proteins and lipids to the Golgi apparatus. The Golgi apparatus can be thought of as the "post office" because it sorts and processes proteins. Ribosomes are the tiny-shaped balls found in the cell that makes the proteins. Cells need proteins to build new structures, repair damage, and direct chemical reactions

Although there are many similarities between plant and animal cells, there are differences too. A plant cell has a cell wall and the animal cell does not. The cell wall is an extra layer that maintains the cell shape.

Also, plant cells have chloroplasts that the animal cell does not have. Chloroplasts help the plant turn light energy from the sun into food for the plant. Plant and animal cells are different in shape and size too. Plant cells are usually larger and rectangular, whereas animal cells are round

PLANT AND ANIMAL CELLS

Week Five

Day 1

Name: _____

Label the Animal Cell.

Word Bank

Endoplasmic Reticulum	Cytoplasm	Golgi Apparatus	Nucleus
Cell Membrane	Ribosomes	Vacuole	Mitochondria

37

©The Discovery Apple LLC

Name: _____

After reading the passage on page 36 about plants and animal cells, answer the following questions.

1. Which of the following is a characteristic of plant cells but not animal cells?

    a)   Nucleus
    b)   Mitochondria
    c)   Vacuole
    d)   Cell Wall

2. Which organelle is responsible for providing energy to the cell?

    a)   Nucleus
    b)   Mitochondria
    c)   Ribosome
    d)   Golgi Apparatus

3. Which organelle is often referred to as the "control center" of the cell?

    a)   Golgi Apparatus
    b)   Endoplasmic Reticulum
    c)   Nucleus
    d)   Vacuole

4. What is the function of the vacuole in plant cells?

    a)   It stores water and nutrients for the cell
    b)   It provides shape and support to the cell
    c)   It helps with the production of energy in the cell
    d)   It controls the movement of substances in and out of the cell.

5. What is the transportation network of the cell called?

    _____

6. What is considered the "post office" of the cell?

    _____

7. What organelle makes proteins?

    _____

8. Why do cells need proteins?

    _____

    _____

Week Five

Name: _____

Organelle Function

Write the function for each organelle. The first one is done for you.

Organelle	Function
Mitochondria	Breaks down food to produce energy for the cell
Cell Membrane	
Vacuole	
Chloroplast	
Golgi Apparatus	
Ribosomes	
Endoplasmic Reticulum	
Nucleus	
Cytoplasm	
Cell Wall	

Week Five

Name: _____

Plant Cell, Animal Cell, or Both?

Classify each statement as belonging to a **plant cell**, an **animal cell**, or **both**.

1.

Has a nucleus

_____

2.

Has a large vacuole

_____

3.

Contains chloroplasts

_____

4.

Has vesicles

_____

5.

Contains mitochondria

_____

6.

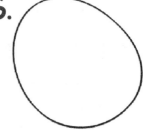

Its shape is round and irregular

_____

Week Five

Name: _____

Imagine you are a plant cell. Describe the importance of chloroplasts in your cell and how they help you survive and grow. How would your cell be different without chloroplasts?

Human Body Systems

Your blood vessels are like highways, transporting oxygen, nutrients, and waste products throughout your body. Did you know that if you stretched out all the blood vessels in your body, they would circle the Earth more than twice?

Name: _____

The Digestive System

Read and gather clues from the passage to label the Digestive System

Did you know that everything you ate for breakfast this morning is being broken down into substances your organs and cells can use? That is the job of your digestive system — breaking down food into nutrients that can be absorbed by the body. Depending on what you eat, it could take your food around 24 hours to go through the digestive system, which is 20 – 30 feet long!

The digestive system begins with the mouth, where food is chewed and mixed with saliva, making it easier to swallow. From there, the food travels down the esophagus and into the stomach. Did you know that your stomach is the about the size of a tennis ball when it is empty and stretches to the size of a football when it is filled with food? Your stomach releases juices and acid that break down the food even more and kills a lot of harmful bacteria so that you don't get sick.

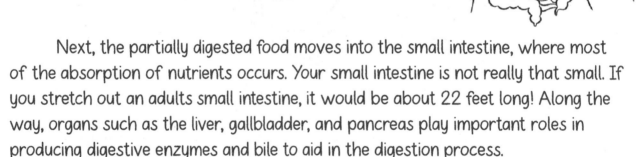

Next, the partially digested food moves into the small intestine, where most of the absorption of nutrients occurs. Your small intestine is not really that small. If you stretch out an adults small intestine, it would be about 22 feet long! Along the way, organs such as the liver, gallbladder, and pancreas play important roles in producing digestive enzymes and bile to aid in the digestion process.

Any remaining undigested food then passes into the large intestine, where water and salts are absorbed, forming solid waste known as feces. The large intestine is fatter than the small intestine, but if you spread it out, it would measure only about 5 feet long.

Finally, any food that the body does not need or can't use later leaves the body as waste through the rectum.

Week Six

Day 1

Name: _____

The Digestive System

Read and gather clues from the passage (page 44) to label the Digestive System.
One is already labeled for you.

Word Bank

Small Intestine	Stomach	Large Intestine	Esophagus
Mouth	Pancreas	Rectum	Liver

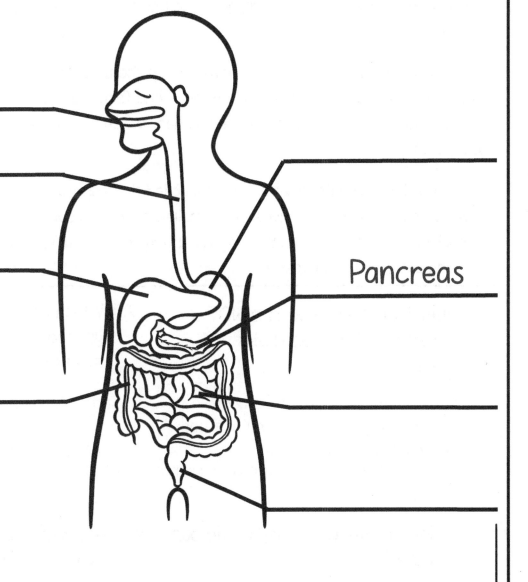

Pancreas

Week Six

Name: _____

The Respiratory System

The respiratory system is an important part of our body because it helps us breathe and exchange gases. When we inhale, air goes in through our nose or mouth, down a tube called the windpipe, and into our lungs. Inside our lungs, there are tiny air pockets called alveoli, where the exchange of gases happens. The oxygen from the air goes into our blood, while the carbon dioxide from our body goes out into the air when we breathe out.

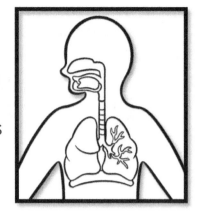

When you breathe out, the air moves up the trachea and flows past the vocal cords. The vocal cords start to vibrate back and forth caused by the moving air. As they vibrate, they make the sound people hear when you speak or sing, also known as your voice.

Breathing is controlled by a muscle called the diaphragm, which moves up and down to help our chest get bigger and smaller, so air can come in and out of our lungs. So, basically, the respiratory system gives us oxygen and takes away the bad gases, so our body can function properly.

---

1. Which of the following is NOT a function of the respiratory system?

   a) Carrying oxygen to the body
   b) Pumping blood throughout the body
   c) Removing waste gases
   d) Helping us speak and produce sounds

2. Which of the following is a waste gas that is released when we exhale?

   a) Oxygen
   b) Nitrogen
   c) Hydrogen
   d) Carbon Dioxide

3. How do we take oxygen into our bodies?

   a) Through our skin
   b) Through our ears
   c) Through our mouth and nose
   d) Through our stomach

4. Which muscle helps us breathe by moving up and down?

   a) Diaphragm
   b) Biceps
   c) Quadriceps
   d) Hamstrings

Name: _____

The Nervous System
Vocabulary Match

Match each word with its definition. Write the correct letter in the space provided.

1. Nervous System _____

2. Brain _____

3. Neuron _____

4. Spinal Cord _____

5. Reflex _____

6. Cerebellum _____

7. Cerebrum _____

8. Nerves _____

9. Medulla _____

10. Impulses _____

(A) A part of your brain located in the back that controls movement, balance, and coordination

(B) An electrical signal carried by nerve cells when stimulated, also known as "action potential"

(C) Thin, fiber-like wires that carry messages from the brain to other parts of the body in order to control our movements

(D) The organ inside the skull that controls al the functions of the body and helps us to think, learn, and remember.

(E) An automatic response to a stimulus without conscious thought

(F) The biggest part of your brain that controls thinking, learning, and feelings, and stores memories.

(G) A long, thin bundle of nerves that runs down the back and carries signals between the brain and the rest of the body

(H) The network of organs and tissues that controls and coordinates the body's actions and responses.

(I) Also known as "brain stem". It controls involuntary muscles like breathing, heartbeat, swallowing, and food digestion.

(J) A specialized cell that transmits electrical signals and carries information throughout the nervous system.

Name: _____

The Skeletal System

Layers of a Bone

There are three main layers of a bone. The outermost layer of bone is a smooth, hard covering that protects its interior. This is called the compact bone. Then, there is the spongy layer which is the soft flexible part of the bone called the spongy bone. The innermost part of the bone is made of a jellylike material called bone marrow. There are two kinds of bone marrow: yellow and red. Red bone marrow is where blood cells are produced. Fat cells usually make up yellow bone marrow

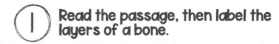

(1) **Read the passage, then label the layers of a bone.**

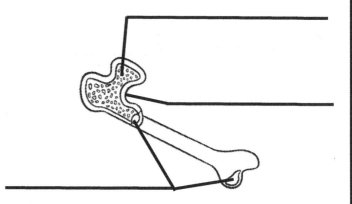

Joints

(2) **Read the passage and use the word bank to label the four movable joints.**

Word Bank	Ball and Socket	Gliding	Hinge	Pivot

All of the bones in your body come together in a very unique way. The places where these bones meet and connect are called joints. There are four main types of movable joints: ball and socket, hinge, pivot, and gliding. The ball and socket joint allows you to move the most freely because of the way it's connected. A good example of this type of joint is your hips and shoulders. Your elbow is an example of a hinge joint because it only moves back and forth in one direction. A pivot joint allows for a twisting and rotating movement so that you can keep your head bobbing to all your favorite songs. The gliding joint can be found in your palms. It lets your bones glide past one another on the flat part of the bone.

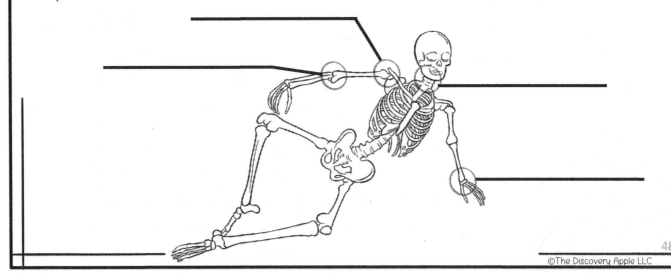

Name: _____

The Circulatory System: Imagine you are running a race, and your heart starts beating faster. Why do you think your heart beats faster during exercise? How does this help your body?

Parts of a Plant

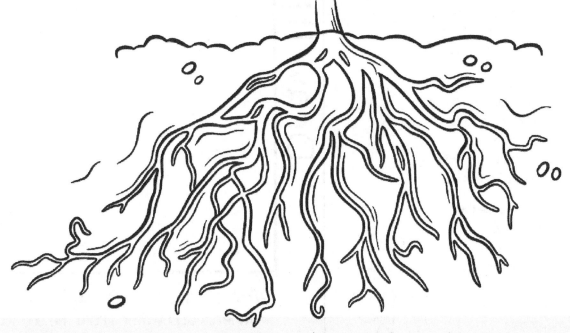

Roots are like the anchor of a plant, keeping it firmly grounded in the soil. They also absorb water and nutrients from the soil, like a straw sucking up a tasty drink!

Week Seven

Name: _____

1. Read the passage
2. Draw and label a plant using the word bank.
3. Answer the questions.

Word Bank | Leaves Stem Fruit Roots Flowers

Plant Structures

Plants have different parts that we call structures. These structures contribute to the plant's life and growth. Roots, stems, leaves, and flowers are the basic structures you can identify in most plants.

Roots grow in the ground, and they have very important functions. They anchor the plant to the ground. They also absorb water and nutrients from the soil to be transported to the rest of the plant. You can find some plants that store the food they make in their roots, like carrots or potatoes.

The plant's **stem** connects the roots to the rest of the plant and holds the leaves, flowers, and fruits upright. The stem is also responsible for carrying the nutrients and water from the roots to other parts of the plant.

Leaves are responsible for making food for the plant by absorbing sunlight. Other than sunlight, they need water and carbon dioxide in order to make sugar for the plant to eat. The process of making food for the plant is called photosynthesis. Have you also noticed the veins that are on most leaves? These veins carry the food the leaf makes to the rest of the plant.

Most plants also have brightly colored **flowers**. The beauty and fragrance of flowers attract pollinators such as bees or butterflies. These pollinators help spread pollen from one flower to another, allowing the flowers to produce seeds. Seeds are very important to plants because new plants can grow from seeds. Without seeds, the growth and survival of many plant species would be limited!

Draw It!

1. What is responsible for sucking up nutrients and water from the soil to the plant?

   a) Fruits
   b) Roots
   c) Stem
   d) Flowers

2. What is responsible for catching sunlight and allowing both air and water to enter the plant?

   a) Stem
   b) Roots
   c) Buds
   d) Leaf

Week Seven

Name: _____

Parts of a Flower
Read the passage and answer the questions.

Flowers come in many different shapes, sizes, and colors, but most of them have a similar basic structure. Petals are often brightly colored and highly scented to attract pollinators such as bees and butterflies.

Sepals are small leaf-like parts found below the petals. Their job is to protect the flower before it blossoms.

The male part of the flower is the stamen. The head of the stamen called the anther is responsible for producing pollen. The filament is the stalk that holds the anther and attaches it to the flower.

The female part of the flower is the pistil. It is made up of the stigma, style, and ovary. The stigma is the head of the pistil that receives the pollen which will begin the process of fertilization.
The style is the name for the stalk of the pistil where the stigma sits. The ovary is the base of the pistil usually at the bottom of the flower. This holds the ovules (eggs) waiting for fertilization which turns into fruits.

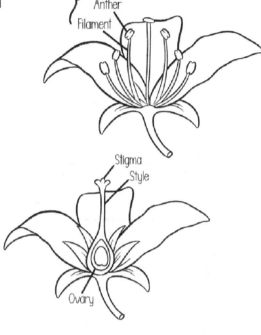

1. Why are petals often brightly colored and highly scented?

   a) To protect the flower from predators
   b) To store food for the plant
   c) To provide structural support
   d) To attract pollinators

2. What is the male part of the flower called?

   a) Stamen
   b) Pistil
   c) Sepal
   d) Patel

3. What is responsible for producing pollen?

   a) Stigma
   b) Anther
   c) Ovary
   d) Style

4. What is the female part of the flower called?

   a) Stamen
   b) Patel
   c) Pistil
   d) Sepal

Name: _____

Parts of a Plant
Vocabulary Match
Match each word with its definition. Write the correct letter in the space provided.

1. Leaves _____

2. Stem _____

3. Seeds _____

4. Roots _____

5. Sepals _____

6. Buds _____

7. Stamen _____

8. Petals _____

9. Pistil _____

A The part of a plant that contains new plants inside it
_____

B The male part of a flower that makes pollen
_____

C Protects the flower before it opens
_____

D Grows on a stem and absorbs sunlight
_____

E The female part of a flower that creates seeds

F Colorful parts of a flower that attracts pollinators

G Grows underground, holds the plant steady, and absorbs water and nutrients from the soil
_____

H Little bumps on the stem that grow into leaves, flowers, and branches
_____

I Holds up the plant and moves water and nutrients from the roots to the leaves, flowers, and fruits

Week Seven

Name: _____

Label the parts of a flower.

WORD BANK

Ovary	Stem	Anther	Style
Sepal	Filament	Ovule	Stigma

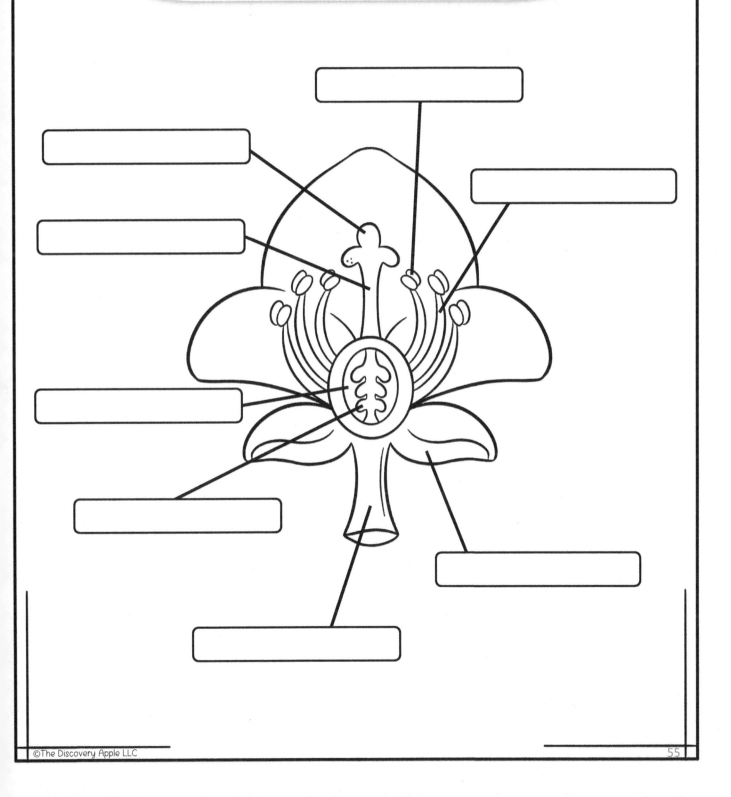

Name: _____

Some plants have thorns or spines on their stems or leaves. Why do you think these plants have developed such adaptations? How might these thorns or spines help the plants in their survival and interaction with other organisms?

Plant Life Cycle

Did you know that bamboo is the fastest growing plant in the world? In fact, bamboo can grow up to 35 inches in just one day!

Week Eight

Name: _____

The Journey of a Plant

It all starts with a tiny seed. When a seed is planted in the soil and absorbs water while being warmed by sunlight, it begins to germinate. Germination is when the seed starts to sprout and grow roots.

As the seed grows, it develops into a seedling. The seedling pushes its way up through the soil, and its tiny leaves begin to unfold. The roots grow deeper into the soil to anchor the plant and absorb water and nutrients.
With time, the seedling grows into a mature plant. It continues to grow taller and wider, producing more leaves, stems, and branches. The plant's main job is to make food through a process called photosynthesis, using sunlight, water, and carbon dioxide.

When a plant reaches maturity, it may produce flowers. Flowers are not only beautiful, but also essential for the plant's reproduction. After pollination, which occurs when pollinators like bees transfer pollen between plants, the flower begins to produce seeds. The seeds contain the genetic information needed to grow into new plants. Some plants scatter their seeds, while others rely on animals or the wind to spread them.

And so, the cycle begins again, with seeds germinating and growing into new plants, continuing the circle of life for plants.

Number the steps of the plant life cycle from 1-6, with 1 being the first stage and 6 being the last.

Flowers begin to bloom on the plant.
_____

The seedling grows above the soil.
_____

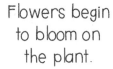 The seed absorbs water _____

Roots start growing out of the seed.
_____

The flowers are pollinated to make seeds.
_____

The plant is growing more stems, leaves, and branches.
_____

Week Eight

Name: _____

Describe each term in your own words and illustrate it with a drawing.

	Explain	Picture
Seed		
Germination		
Seedling		
Young Plant		
Mature Plant		
Pollination		

Week Eight

Name: _____

Plant Life Cycle
Vocabulary Match

Match each word with its definition. Write the correct letter in the space provided.

1. Life Cycle _____

2. Seed _____

3. Germination _____

4. Seedling _____

5. Embryo _____

6. Pollination _____

7. Pollen _____

8. Seed Dispersal _____

9. Reproduce _____

 A The process that takes place when pollinators take pollen between plants to make seeds. _____

 B the small parts produced by plants from which new plants grow _____

 C A sticky powder inside the flower that causes a new plant to form seeds _____

 D The process of a living thing creating another living thing _____

 E When a baby plant grows out of a seed above the soil

 F The stages a plant goes through during its life _____

 G The baby plant inside of a seed _____

H The way seeds get from the parent plant to a new plant _____

I A young plant that has grown above the soil after germinating from a seed

Week Eight

Name: _____

Under each picture, write what you see. Use the word bank.

WORD BANK
Young Plant   Germination   Seed
Pollination   Seedling   Mature Plant

_____   _____   _____

_____   _____   _____

Answer the multiple choice questions.

1. What do seeds need in order to begin to germinate?

   a) Only sunlight
   b) Air, water, and soil
   c) Warm temperatures and nutrients
   d) Pollinators and wind

2. What do the flowers produce through pollination?

   a) Fruits
   b) Leaves
   c) Seeds
   d) Roots

3. When the first sign of plant life appears above the soil we call it a

   a) Flower
   b) Fruit
   c) Seedling
   d) Root

4. What is the stage in the plant life cycle where a new plant begins to grow from a seed?

   a) Pollination
   b) Maturation
   c) Fruition
   d) Germination

Name: _____

Why is pollination an important step in the plant life cycle? How does it contribute to the reproduction and survival of plants?

_____

_____

_____

_____

_____

_____

_____

_____

_____

_____

_____

_____

_____

_____

_____

_____

_____

_____

_____

Photosynthesis

Did you know that one large tree can provide a day's supply of oxygen for up to four people?

Name: _____

Understanding Photosynthesis

It would be weird to see a plant eating food the same way we do, don't you think? The way a plant gets its nutrients to grow and stay alive is a completely different process than that of humans and animals. We call their process of making their own food photosynthesis! Photosynthesis is the process plants use to take the energy from the sun and use it to convert carbon dioxide and water into food. The food they make is called glucose. Glucose is sugar.

The three basic things plants need in order to stay alive are sunlight, carbon dioxide, and water. Without any of these three things, plants will die. If all plants die, we would die too because plants breathe out oxygen, and we need oxygen to breathe. Plants are a major source of oxygen on Earth. While we breathe in oxygen, we also breathe out carbon dioxide. So, we are helping plants too!

The way plants get their energy from sunlight is by a green chemical in the leaves called chlorophyll. Chlorophyll absorbs the sun's energy and it is what gives the leaves their green color.

Plants get water and minerals from the soil through their veins called xylem and goes to the leaves. Next time you want to water a plant, make sure you water their soil! Gardeners use fertilizer to give plants more nutrients because the soil does not always have enough nutrients like nitrogen, phosphorus, and potassium. Some fertilizers are made from chemicals while others are made from natural things like cow poop. That's right — poop is filled with nutrients for plants!

1. True or False. Plants eat food similar to the way humans eat food.

2. What is the process of how plants make their own food called?

_____

3. How do plants make their own food?

_____

_____

_____

4. What is the food that plants make called?

_____

5. What are the three basic things plants need to stay alive?

_____

_____

6. Why would we die if all of the plants in the world die?

_____

_____

_____

7. What absorbs the sun energy?

_____

8. How do plants get water and minerals?

_____

_____

_____

Name: _____

Steps of Photosynthesis

Imagine you are exploring a vibrant garden filled with colorful flowers and tall trees. Have you ever wondered how these plants grow so tall and lush? It is all thanks to the fascinating process called photosynthesis.

It is a sunny day in the garden, and sunlight is what plants need for photosynthesis to work. But how do they capture it? That's where chlorophyll comes in. Chlorophyll is a green pigment found in the leaves of plants absorbing energy from the sun.

Leaves have tiny pores called stomata, and through these tiny openings, plants take in something very important: carbon dioxide. Just like we need oxygen to breathe, plants need carbon dioxide to make food. Meanwhile, down below the ground, the plant's roots are busy getting water from the soil. The water travels up through the stem, all the way to the leaves.

Now the leaves have sunlight, carbon dioxide, and water. Inside the leaves, water and carbon dioxide combine with the energy from sunlight to make a special kind of sugar called glucose. The plant uses some of this glucose for energy to grow and stay healthy. During this time, the plant also releases oxygen into the air for us to breathe, because the plant doesn't need it.

The plant is not wasteful! It stores any extra water and glucose it doesn't need right away in special compartments called vacuoles. This way, it has reserves for later, just in case.

Number the steps of photosynthesis from 1-6, with 1 being the first stage and 6 being the last.

Carbon dioxide enters the leaves of a plant through their tiny holes known as stomata. Water enters the plant through its roots. _____	Sunlight shines on the leaves of a plant and is absorbed by a green pigment called chlorophyll. _____	The plant uses the glucose but releases the oxygen into the air. _____
The water and carbon dioxide combine with the stored energy to make food (glucose) and oxygen. _____	The extra water and glucose are stored in the vacuoles of the plant cells for use later on when needed. _____	Water travels all the way through the stem to reach the leaves. _____

Name: _____

Week Nine

Photosynthesis
Vocabulary Match
Match each word with its definition. Write the correct letter in the space provided.

1. Photosynthesis _____

2. Carbon dioxide _____

3. Oxygen _____

4. Glucose _____

5. Chlorophyll _____

6. Xylem _____

7. Stomata _____

A — Sugar

B — Very thin pores, or holes, in the leaves of plants that are responsible in absorbing carbon dioxide from the air and releasing oxygen back into the air

C — A gas that is absorbed by leaves

D — A green substance in the leaves of plants that absorb sunlight

E — The process plants use to take the energy from sunlight and use it to convert carbon dioxide and water into food

F — The gas plants release into the air that is needed for people and animals to breathe

G — Plant veins which carry water from the roots to all parts of a plant

Week Nine

Name: _____

Photosynthesis Process Labeling

Use the word bank and pay attention to the arrows to label the plant diagram showing the photosynthesis process.

WORD BANK   Carbon Dioxide   Water   Oxygen   Energy

Name: _____

Imagine if plants didn't undergo photosynthesis. How do you think this would impact the availability of oxygen in the atmosphere and the food chain?

Answer keys

Answer Keys

Week One

Food Chains and Food Webs

Page 10 - Day 1

1. Herbivore
2. Decomposer
3. Omnivore
4. Carnivore
5. Carnivore
6. Producer
7. Herbivore
8. Decomposer

Page 11 — Day 2

1. B
2. A
3. C
4. B

Page 12 — Day 3

1. D
2. B
3. C
4. A
5. E
6. The student can choose the animals they want to list under each category. Check to ensure that the animals they list are in the correct category. Additionally, make sure the illustrations they draw represent what the animals they listed actually eat. For example, if the student lists a bunny and an elephant under herbivore, they can draw a picture of a carrot and grass to represent the food these animals eat.

Page 13 — Day 4

1. Phytoplankton and seaweed
2. 8
3. Blue whale and killer whale

Page 14 — Day 5

Example response: When one part of a food chain or food web is disrupted, it can affect other organisms because everything is connected. If one animal disappears, it can make it hard for other animals to find food. If the population of some animals grow too much, it can cause problems for plants. Therefore, it is important to take care of the entire food web to keep the balance in nature.

Week Two

Biomes

Page 16 — Day 1

1. Tundra
2. Rainforest
3. Marine
4. Desert
5. Freshwater
6. Grassland

Page 17 — Day 2

1. D
2. B
3. A
4. C
5. Describe it- (example response): The freshwater biome includes bodies of water such as rivers, lakes, ponds, and streams. You can find plants like algae, mosses, and water lilies, and animals like fish, frogs, and even insects.

Page 18 — Day 3

1. B
2. E
3. A
4. D
5. C
6. The student researches about tropical and temperate rainforests. Here is an example of a filled in chart:

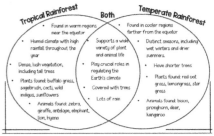

View up-close example — page 75

Page 19 — Day 4

SCAN ME

Page 20 — Day 5

Answers will vary. Here are some examples of questions they might have and what they might want to learn.

- How do desert plants survive with so little water?
- What are some unique adaptations of desert animals? How do they stay cool in the hot desert or how do they find water to drink?
- Are there any special plants or animals in the desert that can only be found there? Are there any rare or endangered species that depend on the desert habitat?

Answer Keys

Week Three

Animal Adaptations

Page 22 - Day 1

1. Instinctive
2. Instinctive
3. Learned
4. Instinctive
5. Learned
6. Learned

Page 23 — Day 2

1. Tusks
2. Trunk
3. To protect them from the sun and insects
4. They are trying to cool off because they are very hot.

Page 24 — Day 3

1. H
2. C
3. G
4. E
5. A
6. F
7. J
8. B
9. I
10. D

Page 25 — Day 4

1. Physical
2. Behavioral
3. Physical
4. Behavioral
5. Behavior
6. Physical

Page 26 — Day 5

Example Response:
Giraffes have really long necks that help them reach leaves high up in the trees. This adaptation helps them find food that other animals can't reach. Another example of an animal with a special wat of getting food is the hummingbird. Hummingbirds have long, skinny beaks that they use to drink nectar from flowers. Their beaks are like straws. They can reach deep into the flowers to get sweet nectar.

Week Four

Animal Classification

Page 28 - Day 1

1. Reptile
2. Amphibian
3. Fish
4. Mammal
5. Bird
6. Insect

Page 29 — Day 2

Answers may vary. Here are example responses:

Warm-blooded animals:
Dog — Mammal
Bald eagle — Bird
Polar bear — Mammal
African Elephant — Mammal
Lion — Mammal

Cold-blooded animals:
Snake — Reptile
Bullfrog — Amphibian
Goldfish — Fish
House Gecko — Reptile
Iguana — Reptile

Page 30 — Day 3

1. F
2. I
3. D
4. A
5. G
6. B
7. J
8. E
9. H
10. C

Page 31 — Day 4

1. Vertebrate
2. Vertebrate
3. Invertebrate
4. Invertebrate
5. Invertebrate
6. Vertebrate

Page 32/33 — Day 5

Response will vary.

Week Five

Plant and Animal Cells

Page 37 — Day 1

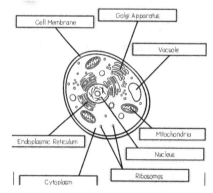

View up-close example — page 75

Answer Keys

Page 38 – Day 2

1. D
2. B
3. C
4. A
5. Endoplasmic Reticulum
6. Golgi Apparatus
7. Ribosomes
8. To build new structures, repair damage, and direct chemical reactions

Page 39 – Day 3

Cell Membrane – The layer that controls what comes in and out of the cell.
Vacuole – Holds water or other materials
Chloroplast – Uses energy from the sun to create food for the plant cell.
Golgi Apparatus – Sorts and processes proteins
Ribosomes – Makes the proteins
Endoplasmic Reticulum – Takes molecules where they need to go
Nucleus – Controls the activities of the cell
Cytoplasm – Holds and protects the cell's organelles
Cell Wall – The layer that gives structure and support in plant cells

Page 40 – Day 4

1. Both
2. Plant Cell
3. Plant Cell
4. Animal Cell
5. Both
6. Animal Cell

Page 41 – Day 5

Example Response:
As a plant cell, chloroplasts play a crucial role in my survival and growth. They contain pigment called chlorophyll, which helps capture sunlight and convert it into energy through a process called photosynthesis. This energy is essential for producing glucose, a type of sugar that provides fuel for various cellular activities. Without chloroplasts, I would not be able to make my own food through photosynthesis, and my growth and survival would be severely affected. I would have to rely on obtaining nutrients from other sources, such as absorbing them from the soil.

Week Six
Human Body Systems

Page 45 – Day 1

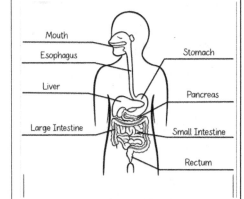

Page 46 – Day 2

1. B
2. D
3. C
4. A

Page 47 – Day 3

1. H
2. D
3. J
4. G
5. E
6. A
7. F
8. C
9. I
10. B

Page 48 – Day 4

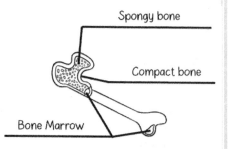

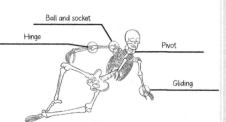

View up-close example – page 76

Page 49 – Day 5

Example response:
My heart beats faster during excercise because my body needs more oxygen and energy. When my heart beats faster, it pumps more blood to my muscles so they can get the oxygen and energy they need to keep running. It helps my body because it gives my muscles the power they need to keep going and helps me run faster. Also, when my heart beats faster, it helps my body get rid of wastes like carbon dioxide more quickly. So my heart beating faster during exercise is important for keeping my body strong and healthy!

Answer Keys

Week Seven

Parts of a Plant

Page 52 – Day 1

Draw It:

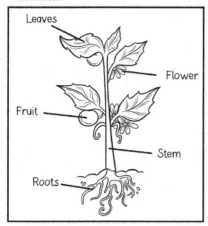

1. B
2. D

Page 53 – Day 2

1. D
2. A
3. B
4. C

Page 54 – Day 3

1. D   7. B
2. I   8. F
3. A   9. E
4. G
5. C
6. H

Page 55 – Day 4

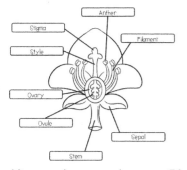

View up-close example – page 76

Page 56 – Day 5

Example Response:
Some plants have thorns or spines to protect themselves from animals that might want to eat them. The thorns or spines make it difficult for animals to get close to the plant or to chew on its leaves. They help the plant survive because animals are less likely to eat them, which means the plant can keep growing and producing seeds. The thorns and spines also help the plant compete with other plants for space and sunlight, because animals might choose to go to plants without thorns or spines instead.

Week Eight

Plant Life Cycle

Page 58 - Day 1

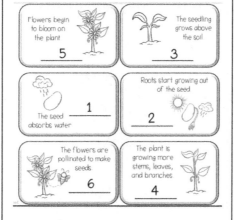

Page 59 – Day 2

The student will describe each term in their own words and draw a picture to show their explanations.
Example responses:
Seed – Seed is like a tiny package that holds a baby plant inside.
Germination – when a seed begins to wake up and sprout
Seedling – a baby plant that has just started to grow
Young plant – bigger than a seedling but still growing and getting ready to become a full-grown plant
Mature plant – fully-grown plant that has reached its maximum size producing flowers, fruits, and seeds
Pollination – how plants make "babies" by transferring pollen from one flower to another

Page 60 – Day 3

1. F   7. C
2. B   8. H
3. E   9. D
4. I
5. G
6. A

Page 61 – Day 4

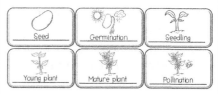

View up-close example – page 77

1. B
2. C
3. C
4. D

Answer Keys

Page 62 — Day 5

Example Response:
Pollination is very important in the plant life cycle because it helps plants make new seeds and grow more plants. When pollination happens, pollen from the male parts of a flower goes to the female parts of another flower. This helps the flower to make seeds, which can grow into new plants. Pollination can happen in different ways, like bees, butterflies, or even the wind. Without pollination, plants wouldn't be able to reproduce and make more plants. So, it is really important for the survival and growth of plants.

Week Nine

Photosynthesis

Page 64 — Day 1

1. False
2. Photosynthesis
3. They take the energy from the sun and use it to convert carbon dioxide and water into food
4. Glucose
5. Sunlight, carbon dioxide, and water
6. Plants breathe out oxygen and we need oxygen to breathe
7. Chlorophyll
8. From the soil through their veins and goes to the leaves

Page 65 — Day 2

View up-close example — page 77

Page 66 - Day 3

1. E
2. C
3. F
4. A
5. D
6. G
7. B

Page 67 - Day 4

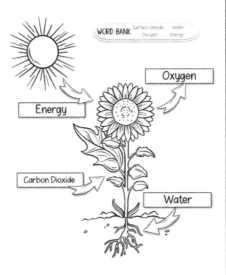

Page 68 - Day 5

Example Response:
If plants didn't undergo photosynthesis, It would have a big impact on the availability of oxygen in the atmosphere and the food chain. Photosynthesis is how plants produce oxygen, and oxygen is important for humans and other animals to breathe. Without photosynthesis, there would be less oxygen in the air, which could make it difficult for living things to survive. Also, plants are an important part of the food chain because they are producers, meaning they make their own food. If plants couldn't undergo photosynthesis, they wouldn't be able to produce food for other organisms.

Page 18 – Day 3

Tropical Rainforest

- Found in warm regions near the equator
- Humid climate with high rainfall throughout the year
- Dense, lush vegetation, including tall trees
- Plants found: buffalo grass, sagebrush, cacti, wild indigos, sunflowers
- Animals found: zebra, giraffe, antelope, elephant, lion, hyena

Both

- Supports a wide variety of plant and animal life
- Play crucial roles in regulating the Earth's climate
- Covered with trees
- Lots of rain

Temperate Rainforest

- Found in cooler regions farther from the equator
- Distinct seasons, including wet winters and drier summers.
- Have shorter trees
- Plants found: red oat grass, lemongrass, star grass
- Animals found: bison, pronghorn, deer, kangaroo

Page 37 – Day 1

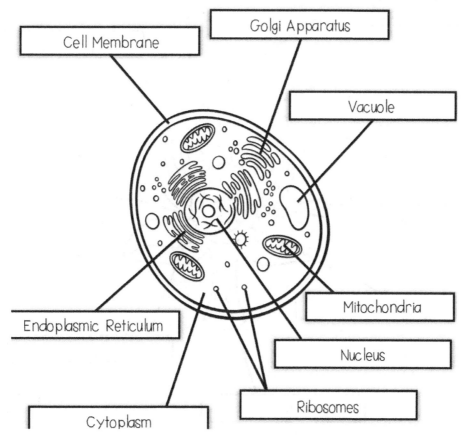

Cell Membrane

Golgi Apparatus

Vacuole

Endoplasmic Reticulum

Mitochondria

Nucleus

Ribosomes

Cytoplasm

Page 48 – Day 4

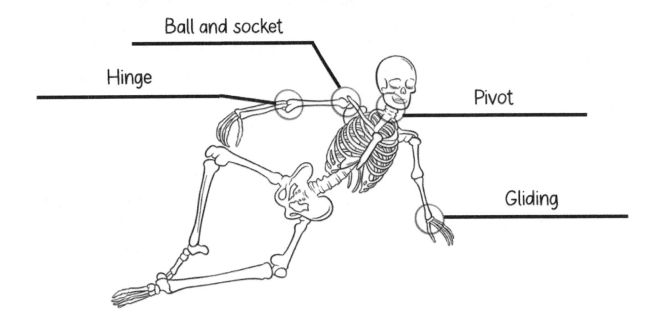

Ball and socket

Hinge

Pivot

Gliding

Page 55 – Day 4

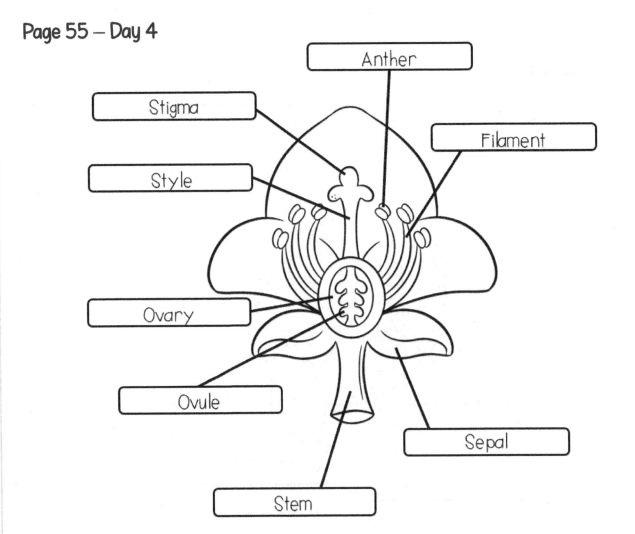

Anther

Stigma

Filament

Style

Ovary

Ovule

Sepal

Stem

Page 61 – Day 4

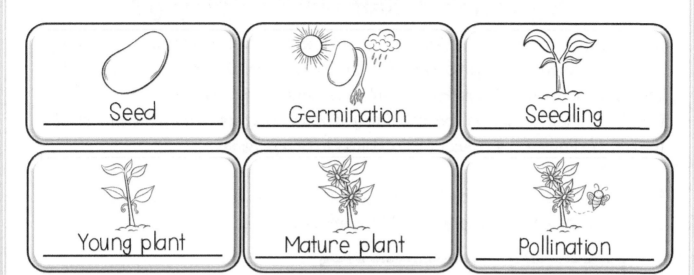

Seed

Germination

Seedling

Young plant

Mature plant

Pollination

Page 65 – Day 2

Carbon dioxide enters the leaves of a plant through their tiny holes known as stomata. Water enters the plant through its roots.

2

Sunlight shines on the leaves of a plant and is absorbed by a green pigment called chlorophyll.

1

The plant uses the glucose but releases the oxygen into the air.

5

The water and carbon dioxide combine with the stored energy to make food (glucose) and oxygen.

4

The extra water and glucose are stored in the vacuoles of the plant cells for use later on when needed.

6

Water travels all the way through the stem to reach the leaves.

3

Looking for more science resources to supplement your child's learning?

Our 'Science Throughout the Year' unit is designed to complement your child's daily science workbook plus additional topics. It provides over 1000 pages and slides of interactive activities, editable PowerPoint slides, lessons, posters, etc. (ALL DIGITAL). Nothing will be mailed to you. You would receive a zip file with all of the editable PowerPoint slides, PDFs, and links to Google Slides.

Reinforce key concepts throughout the year. Simply scan the QR code below to access the unit and enhance your child's science education.

What teachers are saying:

⭐⭐⭐⭐⭐
This resource helped me build confidence to teach science! I've always felt very intimidated and overwhelmed. These resources were so engaging! These made teaching science fun for me, which translated to engagement for my kids! I cannot say thank you enough!

- THE TRAVELING TEXAN TEACHER

⭐⭐⭐⭐⭐
I love this resource! The slides are beautiful and full of information. It is very well organized, the activities are engaging! The children loved all of the activities. I don't know if it had to do anything with this resource but, my students scored so much better on the FCAT than previous classes. Thank you!

- JOANN SO.

⭐⭐⭐⭐⭐
This was one of my best investments this year! My students loved the material and it helped make lesson planning much easier!

-SAMANTHA H.

Contact the Author:
Fatema@thediscoveryapple.com
Contact the Illustrator:
Themagicalgallery@outlook.com

Other workbooks you might like:

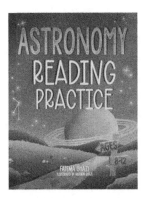

Want Access to my FREE Resource Library?

SCAN ME

All in one place!

Made in United States
North Haven, CT
08 December 2024

61823964R00043